Palos West Media Center
12700 S. 104th Ave.
Palos Park, IL 60464

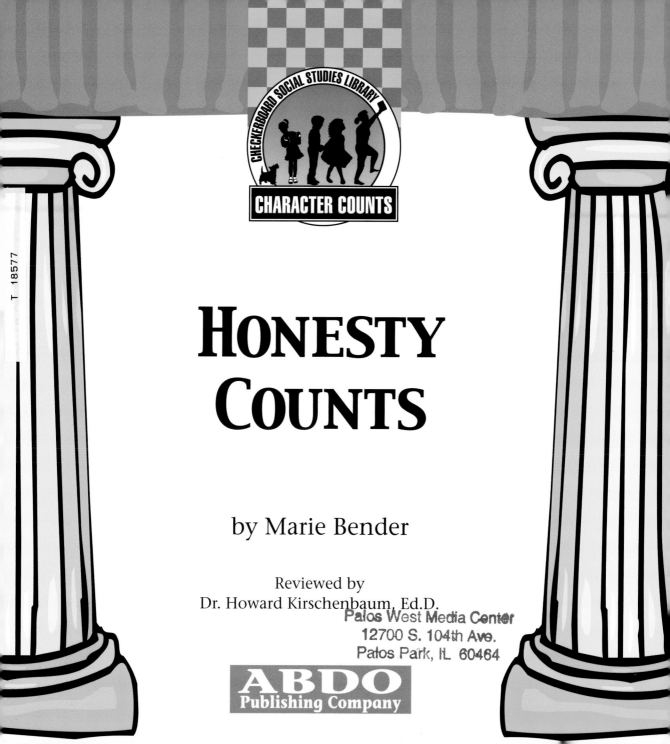

CHECKERBOARD SOCIAL STUDIES LIBRARY

CHARACTER COUNTS

# HONESTY COUNTS

by Marie Bender

Reviewed by
Dr. Howard Kirschenbaum, Ed.D.

**ABDO**
Publishing Company

# visit us at
# www.abdopub.com

Published by ABDO Publishing Company, 4940 Viking Drive, Edina, Minnesota 55435. Copyright © 2003 by Abdo Consulting Group, Inc. International copyrights reserved in all countries. No part of this book may be reproduced in any form without written permission from the publisher.

Printed in the United States.

Photo credits: Brand X Pictures, Comstock, Corbis Images, PhotoDisc, Stockbyte

Editors: Kate A. Conley, Stephanie Hedlund

Design and production: Mighty Media

**Library of Congress Cataloging-in-Publication Data**

Bender, Marie, 1968-
    Honesty counts / Marie Bender.
        p. cm. -- (Character counts)
    Summary: Defines honesty as a character trait and discusses how to be honest at home, with friends, at school, and in the community.
    Includes bibliographical references and index.
    ISBN 1-57765-872-8
    1. Honesty--Juvenile literature. [1. Honesty.] I. Title.

BJ1533.H7 B46 2002
179'.9--dc21

                                                                                2002026148

Internationally known educator and author Howard Kirschenbaum has worked with schools, non-profit organizations, governmental agencies, and private businesses around the world to develop school/family/community relations and values education programs for more than 30 years. He has written more than 20 books about character education, including a high school curriculum. Dr. Kirschenbaum is currently the Frontier Professor of School, Family, and Community Relations at the University of Rochester and teaches classes in counseling and human development.

# CONTENTS

# CHARACTER COUNTS

*All people are created equal.*

*—Thomas Jefferson, third president of the United States*

Your character is the combination of **traits** that makes you an individual. It's not your physical traits, such as the color of your eyes or how tall you are. Rather, character is your thoughts, feelings, beliefs, and values.

Your character shows in the way you interact with your family, friends, teachers, and other community members. People who are well liked and successful are said to have a good character. Many traits build good character. Some of these traits include caring, fairness, honesty, good citizenship, responsibility, and respect.

# Honesty Counts

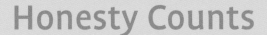

Anna had earned fifteen dollars taking care of her neighbors' cat while they were on vacation. She went to the music store to get a CD. The CD cost twelve dollars. She gave the cashier her fifteen dollars. Anna took the change and the CD and left the store.

When Anna got home, she realized that instead of three one-dollar bills, the cashier had given her two ones and a five! The five must have gotten mixed in with the ones and the cashier hadn't noticed. At first, Anna thought that it wasn't her fault that she got too much change. The cashier gave it to her, so why shouldn't she keep it?

Then Anna noticed that she felt differently about the extra money she got from the cashier than she did about the money she got for cat-sitting.

She was proud that she had earned the money cat-sitting. The extra change from the store didn't make her feel proud. It made her feel sneaky, even though it wasn't her mistake. So Anna went back to the store and explained what had happened. The cashier took the five-dollar bill back, gave her the one-dollar bill she should have been given, and thanked her for being honest.

Anna made honesty count. ■

# WHAT IS HONESTY?

*Liars are not believed even when they tell the truth.*

—Aesop, Greek writer

Honesty is telling the truth and doing what you say you will do. Honest people tell the truth and admit when they make mistakes. They keep the promises they make so others will believe in them. They also follow the rules and do not cheat or steal.

# HONESTY

There are different ways to show you are honest. One way is to be **sincere**. Being sincere is being honest and truthful about what you think and feel, even if other people disagree with you. Agreeing with people just to be liked is insincere.

Being fair is another way to show that you are an honest person. This means you are committed to doing the right thing, even if it would be easier not to do anything. For example, if someone is being blamed for doing something wrong but you saw who really did it, you can speak up and tell the truth. When you tell the truth, you hope that others will be honest in return.

Another way to show you are an honest person is to be trustworthy. Trustworthy people follow the rules and do what they say they will do. If they make a mistake, they admit it and accept the **consequences**. You do not have to be perfect to be trustworthy, you just have to be honest. When you keep your promises and tell the truth, everyone you come in contact with will trust and respect you.

Think about it...

*Do you always tell the truth?*

*What have you said or done recently that shows honesty?*

# Why Should You Be Honest?

 Telling the truth shows you are willing to be responsible for your mistakes.

 Speaking the truth can keep others from being blamed for something they did not do.

 Telling the truth shows you are trustworthy.

 Telling the truth makes you feel good about yourself.

 You want others to be honest with you.

HONESTY

# HONESTY AND FAMILY

*That's the trouble with a lie. You've got to keep adding to it*
*to make it believable to people.* —Bertrand R. Brinley, author

There are many ways to show your family you are honest. For example, do not let your brother take the blame when you break something. Instead, admit to your parents that you did it.

Your family may not always like what you do or say. But lying or saying

what you think they want to hear usually makes the situation worse. Telling the truth does not mean others will not get angry with you, but they will appreciate your honesty.

Honesty within your family makes sure that everyone trusts each other. When your parents go out, don't ask the baby-sitter to let you do things that you know you are not allowed to do. If you tell your little sister that you will read her a story, don't go out to play with your friends instead. Don't sneak into your sister's room and read her diary because snooping is dishonest.

Showing your parents that you are honest is a great way to earn **privileges**. For example, if they know that you tell the truth about where you go and you come home when you are supposed to, they will probably let you go out more often. On the other hand, if you lie about where you have been and come home late, then they might not let you go again. You have not earned their trust because you did not do what you said you would.

Being honest at home is a way to practice being fair, **sincere**, and **genuine** to others and to yourself. It may be hard to be honest all of the time, but telling the truth is important to having good character.

*Think about it...*

*Have you ever lied to your parents?*

*How did you feel when you lied?*

*How did your parents react when they found out you had lied to them?*

*How would the situation have been different if you had told the truth?*

# HONESTY AND FRIENDS

*Sure, over the years [Mongoose and Weasel] had told their share of lies, both of them. Who didn't? But never had they lied to each other. Till now. And it hurt.* —Jerry Spinelli, author

Honesty is an important part of friendship. It can be shown in many ways. An honest person admits to losing or breaking a friend's toy and offers to replace it with a new one or one of his or her own. An honest person returns the book he or she borrowed from a friend after reading it. An honest person doesn't cheat in order to win but follows the rules and tries to win honestly. When a friend tells a secret, an honest person doesn't tell it to anyone else.

If you are afraid that people will not like you, you might make up stories to make yourself seem more interesting. But trying to impress people by lying is dishonest. This behavior is not **genuine**,

**Think about it…**

*Have you ever lied to impress someone or be accepted?*

*Did it work?*

*How did you feel about it later?*

*What did you learn from the experience?*

and your lies will probably be discovered. Not only will your friends feel bad about being lied to, you will lose their trust and respect. This is not a good way to make or keep friends.

It is also important to be **sincere** with your friends. For example, don't tell someone you like basketball, even though you really don't, just because you want him or her to like you. It's good to have some of the same interests as your friends, but you are different people and will like and dislike different things. Friends accept that other people have the **right** to have different opinions. The best way to make friends is to be sincere and show others the real you. Your true friends will like you for who you are, just as you like them for who they are.

# HONESTY

# HONESTY AND SCHOOL

*Repetition does not transform a lie into a truth.*

—*Franklin D. Roosevelt, thirty-second president of the United States*

Honesty at school means being fair and respectful to your teachers and classmates. An honest person shows leadership and responsibility. There are many ways to show you are honest and trustworthy at school.

A common form of dishonesty in school is cheating. Copying information from an encyclopedia, getting your **sibling** to do your homework, or looking at another student's answers during a test are all forms of dishonesty. It might seem like it is worth it to get a better grade. However, if you cheat instead of learning the material for the first test, you will have to learn twice as much by the next test, or continue to cheat. And if you keep cheating instead of learning, then you will never learn what you are supposed to know. And you will not feel very good about yourself.

Think about it...

*Have you ever been tempted to cheat?*

*How would you feel if you were caught cheating?*

*How would you feel if someone cheated off you?*

It is important to tell the truth to people at school. If you did not finish your homework, do not tell your teacher that a bully stole it from you on your way to school. Admit that you did not do it and offer to stay in at recess to finish the assignment.  Or, turn it in late and accept the **consequences**. Sometimes, something happens that interferes with homework, and you have to make a choice. If you choose not to do your homework for a specific reason, it is your decision.  Being honest about it will show the teacher you are truthful and **sincere**.

Making up or spreading **rumors** about other students is dishonest and disrespectful. It hurts others and causes stress. If someone tells you a rumor about a classmate, stand up for your classmate by explaining that spreading rumors hurts people's feelings.

Not taking things that do not belong to you is another way to be honest and trustworthy at school. If you forgot your pencil, you do not just take one out of a classmate's desk. Instead, ask if you can borrow a pencil. If you find another student's jacket on the playground, return it to the owner, or turn it in to the lost and found. It

*What do you do when someone tells you a rumor?*

*How have you felt when you have been the one others are talking about?*

is dishonest to keep it, even if it fits you perfectly and is your favorite color. If you lose your math book, do not take one out of another student's locker. Admit your mistake, and replace it by buying another one. When you take things without asking permission, you are stealing.

When you are an honest and truthful person, others will trust you and look to you as a leader. Teachers, other adults, classmates, and friends will know they can count on you to do what you say you will. Your **sincerity** will inspire others to follow your example to be honest.

HONESTY

# HONESTY AND COMMUNITY

*Honesty is the best policy.*

—Cervantes, Spanish writer

B eing honest in your community means following laws and accepting the **consequences** if you break them. For example, you may accidentally break your neighbor's window while playing baseball. Trying to avoid the consequences by lying or blaming someone else only makes the situation worse. Your neighbor will be upset because the window is broken, but he or she will be even more upset if you lie about it.

When you are in trouble, it is best to admit your mistakes right away and apologize. You will still have to pay the consequences. But you will also be earning respect by handling the situation with honesty.

There are many other ways to be honest in your community. Taking things that do not belong to you is stealing. Sometimes it may seem

*When you have made mistakes, have you handled the situation honestly?*

*What did you do?*

*How did it make you feel?*

# HONESTY

as if it would be easy to steal and that no one would notice. But it is wrong to take what is not yours. Being dishonest does not make you feel good about yourself. If you see someone drop something on the sidewalk, you can pick it up and return it to the person. If you see a bicycle you like in the hall by your neighbor's apartment door, you can **admire** it and talk to your parents about buying your own bicycle. Likewise, you do not steal candy from a store. Instead, you can pay for it with your allowance.

Think about it...

*Have you ever stolen something?*

*How did it make you feel?*

*Has anyone ever stolen something from you?*

*How did you feel?*

# Being Honest with Yourself

*To thine own self be true.* —*William Shakespeare, playwright*

Yes, it is possible to lie to yourself. People tend to do this when they want to avoid taking responsibility for something, or to excuse something they know is wrong. When you tell yourself that you'll clean your room tomorrow, but know you won't because that's what you've said every day for a week, you are lying to yourself.

You also lie to yourself by ignoring or denying the facts. For example, you know it's unsafe to ride your bike without a helmet. But if you tell yourself you'll be okay without a helmet because you're only going a couple of blocks, you are lying to yourself.

If you're lying to yourself, you might make an excuse for something you've done, failed to do, or want to do. For example, you might tell yourself you would have studied for the math test but couldn't because you had to mow the lawn. However, the excuse will only delay the **consequences** of your mistake—in this case, a bad grade.

*Can you think of a lie you've told yourself recently?*

# HONESTY

If you're excusing something that you want to do but know is wrong or unwise, then ask yourself if going to the trouble of thinking up the excuse made your actions worth it. You'll probably find that having to excuse something takes a lot of the fun out of it.

# LITTLE LIES

*Truth is like the sun. You can shut it out for a time, but it ain't goin' away.*

*—Elvis Presley, singer and actor*

Sometimes there is a fine line between being polite and being honest. Using good manners means you thank people whenever they give you something or do something for you. But what if they give you something you do not like? Is thanking them honest? Is not thanking them rude? One way to be honest and polite is to thank the person for thinking of you. Even if you dislike the gift, you do honestly appreciate the thought, so it is not lying to say so.

Some people think it's okay to tell little lies to be polite or to avoid hurting someone's feelings. But it is not right to be dishonest no matter what the situation. It is better to figure out a truthful response or action. Lying can make you feel guilty. Lies can also backfire if someone finds out, or if you have to tell more lies to cover up the first lie you told. Soon, you will wish you had told the truth in the beginning.

**What was the last little lie you told?**

**Can you think of other types of social lies people tell to be polite?**

# HONESTY

It seems that the world is full of lies. When you watch television or read magazines, the commercials and advertisements do not seem totally honest or truthful. Words and pictures give you messages to buy something, use something, or think a certain way. Words such as *always*, *never*, and *100 percent positive* may not be true. It is hard to know what is honest when you are surrounded by misleading messages.

To be true to yourself and to others, it is best to tell the truth. You can learn ways to be honest in situations that could hurt other people's feelings. Think about what you say and practice saying positive things without lying. Others will trust and admire the real you. You will inspire others to be truthful, **sincere**, and **genuine**. You will feel good about yourself by being an honest person.

# The Golden Rule
## Around the World

Hurt not others in ways that you yourself would find hurtful. —Buddha

So whatever you wish that men would do to you, do so to them; for this is the law and the prophets. —*The Gospel of Matthew*

Do not do to others what you do not want them to do to you. —Confucius

Do naught unto others which would cause you pain if done to you. —*The Mahabarata*

No one of you is a believer until he desires for his brother that which he desires for himself. —Muhammad

What is hateful to you, do not to your fellow man. —*The Talmud*

Regard your neighbor's gain as your own gain, and your neighbor's loss as your own loss. —Tai Shang Kan Ying P'ien

# Glossary

**admire** - to think of with respect or approval.

**consequence** - something that results from an earlier action or happening; outcome.

**genuine** - actually being what it seems.

**privilege** - a special right or benefit.

**right** - a legal or moral claim to something.

**rumor** - a story passed from person to person without any evidence to support it.

**sibling** - a brother or sister.

**sincere** - true and honest.

**trait** - a quality that distinguishes one person or group from another.

# Web Sites

Would you like to learn more about character? Please visit www.abdopub.com to find up-to-date Web site links about caring, fairness, honesty, good citizenship, responsibility, and respect. These links are routinely monitored and updated to provide the most current information available.

# INDEX

**C**

caring 4

character traits 4

cheating 8, 14, 18

classmates 18, 20, 21

community 4, 22

**F**

fairness 4, 9, 12, 18

family 4, 11

feelings 4, 9, 16, 18, 20, 24, 27, 29

friends 4, 14, 16, 21

**G**

good citizenship 4

**H**

honesty 4, 8, 9, 11, 12, 14, 18, 20, 21, 22, 24, 27, 29

**L**

laws 22

lying 11, 12, 14, 16, 22, 25, 27, 29

**M**

manners 27

**N**

neighbors 22, 24

**P**

parents 11, 12, 24

**R**

respect 4, 9, 16, 18, 20, 22

responsibility 4, 18, 25

rules 8, 14

rumors 20

**S**

school 18, 20

siblings 11, 12, 18

stealing 8, 20, 21, 22, 24

**T**

teachers 4, 18, 20, 21

For the Character Counts series, ABDO Publishing Company researched leading character education resources and references in an effort to present accurate information about developing good character and why doing so is important. While the title of the series is Character Counts, these books do not represent the Character Counts organization or its mission. ABDO Publishing Company recognizes and thanks the numerous organizations that provide information and support for building good character in school, at home, and in the community.